The Secret Life of

The Secret Life of

The Secret Life of

The Secret Life of

The Secret Life of

C000053555

# The Secret Life of Cats

ROWAN BARNES-MURPHY

summersdale

# THE SECRET LIFE OF CATS

Summersdale Publishers Ltd
46 West Street
Chichester
West Sussex
PO19 1RP
UK

www.summersdale.com

Printed and bound in China

ISBN: 978-1-84953-354-6

Substantial discounts on bulk quantities of Summersdale books are available to corporations,
professional associations and other organisations. For details contact Nicky Douglas by telephone:
+44 (0) 1243 756902, fax: +44 (0) 1243 786300 or email: nicky@summersdale.com.

TO..........................................................

FROM......................................................

*For Frankie, my biggest critic*
*and best friend, with love*

They may appear to be cool, calm and collected, but have you ever wondered how cats behave while you're out of the house? The frisky felines in this book prove that while the owner's away the *cats* will play, and get up to all manner of marvellous mischief, such as…

*... making a splash*

in your very best shoes...

... dealing with all those

*unwanted leftovers...*

*...feline fabulous*

in your finest jewellery...

… selfishly using up all of your

*luxury bathing products…*

… sampling a bottle or two of
your best *Chat O'Neuf*…

… throwing a *cocktail party,* with music courtesy of your most treasured vinyls…

... perfecting a flawless

*feline up-do...*

... whipping up a delectable

*fish cake*...

*...befriending* your pet bird...

...*glamming up*
for the Pussycats' Ball...

… breaking out the ride-on mower for *a bit of fair play* on the lawn…

… rocking the house with a

*tinkle on the ivories*

and a few jars of home brew…

… shaping up with a hearty

round of *swingball*…

... putting your

*new tackle*

through its paces...

… putting on a fashion show for the

local *glamour pusses*…

*... breaking in* your new

5-iron at the local pitch and putt...

*... cooking up a storm*

with your best pots and pans…

… ensuring Rover's

safety and well-being

*at all times…*

… dining *al fresco* with

the rest of the gang…

… indulging in some indoor sports, *feline style…*

… patiently waiting for the

*odd snack* to pass by…

...knitting a *cuddly catsuit* out of your best mohair...

...having some *harmless fun* with an old buddy...

… assisting with *holiday arrangements*…

... *firing up* the barbie

for some fun in the sun...

... strumming the night away with *a lively crowd* of feline fans...

... keeping on top of canine
*sanitation duties...*

... or even enjoying a little

*afternoon delight*

with a close companion!

So next time you pop out to the shops, pay a visit to Granny or spend an evening at a nice restaurant, consider stashing your favourite shoes, padlocking the fridge and bubble-wrapping the budgie – it might just be the day your cat indulges in one of the many activities in its saucy, sneaky, secret life!

If you're interested in finding out more about our humour books, follow us on Twitter: *@summersdaleLOL*

www.summersdale.com